Water Sports
An Outdoor Adventure Handbook

Water Sports
An Outdoor Adventure Handbook

Hugh McManners

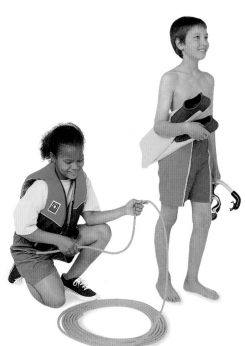

A DK PUBLISHING BOOK

Editor Patricia Grogan **Art Editor** Lesley Betts
Photography Andy Crawford, Gary Ombler, James Jackson

Production Josie Alabaster

US Editor Camela Decaire

Managing Editor Jane Yorke
Managing Art Editor Chris Scollen

Water sports consultant Keith Jennings

The water sports adventurers:
George Bailey, Rachel Butterworth,
Nicholas Culligan, Tanneka Ducille, Rachel Rogers,
Darren Whitehead

First American Edition 1997
2 4 6 8 10 9 7 5 3 1

Published in the United States by DK Publishing, Inc.
95 Madison Avenue, New York, New York 10016

Visit us on the World Wide Web at
http://www.dk.com

Published in Great Britain by Dorling Kindersley Ltd.

A CIP catalog record for this book is available from the Library of Congress.

ISBN 0-7894-1479-1

Color reproduction by Colourscan, Singapore
Printed in Hong Kong by Wing King Tong

Contents

How to use this book

This book contains all the information you need for safe adventures in and on water. It shows you how to paddle, row, and steer all kinds of boats and is packed full of usef hints, tips, and ideas. Enjoy your water sports adventures!

Being safe in the water

Water sports adventures are fun and safe when you are properly prepared. You need to feel confident in the water so that you can cope in any situation. This section shows you how to improve your survival and swimming skills.

Find out how
make a bag for
gear on page

Learn how to n
an emergency f
on page 9.

See page 10 to
learn how to stop
your snorkel mask
from misting up.

Learn how to
perform a duck-
dive on page 13.

Underwater adventures

A snorkel, mask, and fins will enable you to snorkel underwater without needing to come up for air. Learn how to snorkel in a swimming pool and then you can have exciting underwater adventures, including swimming through an obstacle course.

Afloat on your raft

All watercraft have the ability to float, or be buoyant. Make a raft from everyday materials to learn how watercraft stay afloat and then make your own paddles to propel and steer the raft. You can also attach a flag with your own special emblem to the raft.

Learn how to p
your raft or
page 18.

See page 17 to
out about diffe
life jackets.

Learn how to
capsize safely in a
kayak on page 24.

See page 27
to make a sail
on your canoeing
day trip.

Paddling, day trips, and rowing

Canoes are paddled and rowboats are rowed. This section teaches you the differences between these techniques and how to maneuver your craft. Instructions on how to launch and moor your craft will help prepare you for a day trip.

Sailing a sailboat

All sailboats are moved by the wind. An Optimist is the simplest kind, and therefore the best one in which to learn the skills of sailing. Learn all the basic equipment terms and you're ready to set off. When learning, always sail at a boat club.

Find out how
tack on page

Discover why
should always s
off sailing into
wind on page

earn how to
easure water-
th on page 37.

ee page 39 to
arn how to tie
nooring knot.

Charts and nautical knots

All sailors need to know how to read
special maps called charts. By learning how
to read a chart, you can find out the depth
of the water you are sailing on and about
any underwater obstacles. It is equally
important to learn the main nautical knots.

Finding out more

Many people enjoy water sports, so the
water is often crowded. You must learn
basic water rules and be considerate.
Why not contact the national
association for your preferred activity
and join a club recommended by it?

Look up useful
terms in the glossary
on page 46.

Use the index on
page 48 to find
everything in
this book.

v to use each page

page in this book explains
hing you need to know for
adventure. The introduction
you an overview, and the step-
p instructions show you how to
make, and do all the activities.

Knot symbol
You will see this
symbol when
you need to
tie a knot.

Star symbol
This symbol
appears next
to important
safety points.

Direction arrow
The arrow shows
the direction in
which the wind and
craft are moving.

pictures
structions underneath these
s explain how to make
the activities.

or picture
are appears
top left-hand
of each page.
s up what is
covered on
ge.

ages have
n showing
terials or
nent you
ed for
dventure.

*The colored
band on each
page reminds you
which section you
are in. This page
is in the* Paddling,
day trips, and
rowing *section.*

Boat symbol
This symbol
appears next
to useful tips.

Hints and tips
Each hints and tips
box is packed full of
useful information.

*Hints and tips boxes
have a picture of a
boy or girl. Most
pages have one of
these boxes.*

Extra information
At the bottom of most right-hand
pages, you will find additional or
new information about the subject.

Water confidence

Before trying any water sport, you must fe
confident in the water. Practice swimmin
the length of an Olympic pool – 164 ft
(50 m) – treading water for two minutes,
swimming underwater for 30 seconds,
and making an emergency float so
that you can cope in any situation.

Keep your water-adventure gear in a handy bag.

Materials for the bag

Safety pin

Needle

Thread

Cord

Scissors

Oblong piece of material

Hints and tips

Apart from when swimming and snorkeling, you should always wear a life jacket near and on the water.

If your eyes are sensitive, wear goggles to protect them in the water.

Always test your water confidence in a swimming pool.

Dressed for swimming

All you need for swimming adventures
is a swimsuit, a pair of waterproof shoes
to protect your feet, and a towel.

When you get out of the water, dry yourself with a towel. This will stop you from getting cold.

Rinse out your swimsuit each time you wear it to make it last longer.

If you plan to go in and out of the water often, take an extra towel.

Always wear sunblock on sunny days, especially when you are in the water.

Waterproof shoes will protect your feet from rough ground.

See page 38 to learn how to tie a figure-eight knot.

How to make a
from an oblong
of material

Fold the material in
Fold over the top e
1 in (3 cm) and sew
down securely.

Sew up the bottom
one side to make a
shape. Do not sew
the folded edge.

Attach a safety pin
3 ft (1 m) of cord.
the cord through th
folded edge.

Remove the safety p
and tie the two end
cord together with a
figure-eight knot.

v to make an emergency float

ce making a float from a pair of light-
t pants. This skill will not only improve
water confidence, it will also help you
e in an emergency.

1 Practice treading water without using your hands so that you feel comfortable when making the float. Soak the pants in the water and tie a half-hitch knot in the end of each leg.

2 Hold the pants open by the waistband. Take a breath and throw the pants behind your head. You may bob under the water, so keep holding your breath in case this happens. Kick hard with your legs to stay afloat.

See page 39 to learn how to tie a half-hitch knot.

3 Keep hold of the waist-
band in both hands.
hrow the pants up and
ver your head to catch
much air as possible in
e legs. Repeat until the
ant-legs are full of air.

4 Hold the waistband closed and pull it just below the surface of the water. Rest your chin on your hands and let the float hold you up. You only need to kick your legs very gently now to stay afloat.

Many organizations offer life-saving courses that can teach you more survival techniques.

Snorkeling is the perfect way to explore the underwater world.

Snorkeling underwater

A snorkel, mask, and fins will enable you to swim underwater like a fish. The snork helps you breathe while underwater, the m lets you see where you are going, and the allow you to glide easily through the wate When learning to snorkel, practice in a swimming pool with an experienced adult

Equipment

Mask

Snorkel

Fins

Getting ready

Before you start snorkeling, make sure your equipment fits you properly.

1 The edge of the mask should form an airtight seal around your face. When breathing in through your nose, a well-fitting mask will stay on without the strap.

2 Pull the strap over your head to help keep the mask in the correct place. Adjust the length of the strap until it feels comfortable.

3 Attach the snorkel to the looped strap on the mask, see right. Bite lightly on the two rubber stumps in the snorkel mouthpiece and put the rubber plate between your teeth and lips.

How to adjust mask and stop it misting up

To adjust the lengt the strap, pull the t through the unders of the mask.

When swimming underwater, the ma will mist up. To av this, spit into the m

Smear the spit over inside of the mask. a little water aroun the mask to clean it

To keep your snork at the correct angle, the snorkel through looped strap on the

rt breathing

norkel tube
d lie against one
f your head,
to your temple.
sure the tube is
d backward so
clears the water.
ing in shallow
try using the
el by breathing
gh your mouth.
practice, you will
not to breathe
rough your nose.

Temple

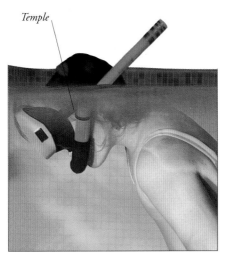

How to clear your mask and snorkel of water

To clear water from your mask, come to the surface first.

Ease the lower-edge seal away from your face and the water will pour out of your mask.

perfect position

ming underwater with fins
practice. Keep your head
and your arms by your sides.
keep your legs fairly straight
ck your feet without raising
ins above the surface.

⭐ Never snorkel alone. Always snorkel with at least two other people.

If your snorkel fills with water, come to the surface and blow out firmly through your mouth.

Practice makes perfect

Moving underwater in fins is called finning. Hold on to the edge of the swimming pool and practice finning. If you can hear your fins breaking the surface, angle your body more.

Try to keep your legs as straight as possible and fin from your hips.

ctice swimming at
fferent depths so
u learn how deep
n go before your
fills with water.

Bend your knees slightly with each kick.

Keep your arms by your sides to help you glide through the water efficiently.

Look ahead so that you can see where you are going.

With experience, you can dive down to the bottom in your snorkel gear.

Exploring the bottom

When you feel confident snorkeling along the water's surface, you can try snorkeling with your snorkel fully underwater, too. This will enable you to explore riverbeds, shorelines, and lake bottoms. You could also make a snorkel bag to hang around your waist to store your finds in.

Materials for the snorkel bag

Thread

Strip of strong material

Velcro

Needle

Scissors

Oblong of net

Cord

Going up and down

Practice holding your breath for one minute and then learn these techniques for moving safely up and down through the water.

Diving feet first

This is the safest way to move down through the water. Keep yourself upright. Point your fins downward and sweep your arms up above your head to push you down through the water.

A raised arm warns other people that you are surfacing.

Coming back to the surface

As soon as you start to run out of breath, come back to the surface. Tilt your body upward and raise one hand above your head. As you come up through the water, your raised hand will warn others that you are surfacing.

Hints and tips

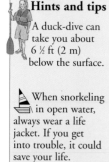

A duck-dive can take you about 6 ½ ft (2 m) below the surface.

When snorkeling in open water, always wear a life jacket. If you get into trouble, it could save your life.

How to make snorkel bag to s your finds i

Fold the net in half up the long edges. cord in and out of end of the short ed

Tie a figure-eight k in both ends of the Knot the cord at th bottom of the net.

Weave another piec cord around the top this cord to the firs with a figure-eight

Close the top of the by pulling the cord and securing it with half-hitch knot.

ow to make a
and attach the
orkel bag to it

out 20 in (60 cm)
erial. Sew the hook-
two Velcro strips to
d of the material.

e eye-side of the
strips to the other
the material.
he strips evenly.

e material through
d on the bag. Wrap
around your waist
ure the Velcro.

page 38 to
n how to tie a
re-eight knot
ge 39 to tie a
ch knot.

Performing a duck-dive

When you have learned to dive feet-first, try duck-diving.
You should find this skill easier to perfect than feet-first
diving, and you will be able to go deeper in the water, too.

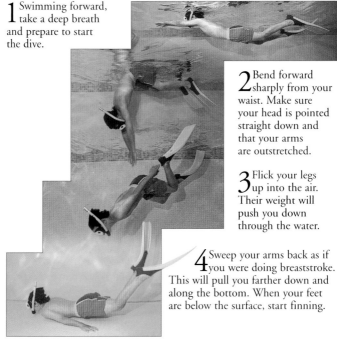

1 Swimming forward,
take a deep breath
and prepare to start
the dive.

2 Bend forward
sharply from your
waist. Make sure
your head is pointed
straight down and
that your arms
are outstretched.

3 Flick your legs
up into the air.
Their weight will
push you down
through the water.

4 Sweep your arms back as if
you were doing breaststroke.
This will pull you farther down and
along the bottom. When your feet
are below the surface, start finning.

Moving along the bottom

Fin underwater for as long as you feel
comfortable. As soon as you start to feel
short of breath, surface and clear your
snorkel. With practice, you will be able to
stay underwater for longer periods of time.

Use the Velcro
strips to make
the belt tighter or
looser for comfort.

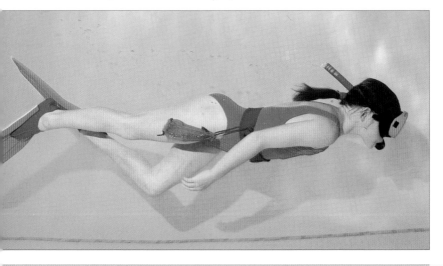

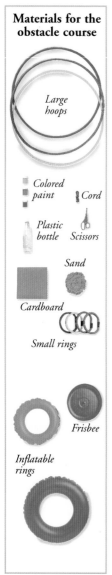

Set up obstacle course competitions with your friends to test your skills.

Underwater obstacles

Making an underwater obstacle course is perfect way to develop your snorkeling sk Once you have made your obstacles, you need to dive down in the water to positio them. This will help you get used to hold your breath, moving up and down throug the water, and carrying objects.

The parts of your course

You can vary your obstacle course depending on what you have at home. However, for safety, never use heavy objects or obstacles in which you could get trapped.

You could friend to you to see ho it takes to com the course.

Swimming through a hoop
Always swim slowly and smoothly through a hoop so that you do not hurt yourself. See page 15 to learn how to weigh the hoop down in the water.

This obstacle will teach you how to fin in a straight line without kicking your legs too far apart.

Inflated rings are useful for adding variety to your course.

How to weigh down a hoop with a plastic bottle and sand

Pour a little paint inside the plastic bottle. Shake the bottle to cover it in paint. Leave it to dry.

Using a marker

You could use a ring as a marker. Raise one hand through the ring before moving on to the next obstacle.

Make a cone by rolling one end of the cardboard and sealing it with tape. Fill the bottle with sand.

Place small objects on a frisbee and then dive down to collect them.

...g for small objects

...ine this obstacle with other parts of ...ourse. You could move a small ring ...ne obstacle to another or dive down ...ect two small objects at a time.

Get 3 ft (1 m) of cord. Loop the middle of the cord around the bottom of the bottle.

Bring the cord to the top of the bottle and wrap it around the lid. Secure the cord with a reef knot.

Bring the cord around the hoop. Tie the ends of the cord together with another reef knot.

 See page 39 to learn how to tie a reef knot.

When near water, always wear a life jacket.

Building a raft

By building a raft you will discover how a boat floats. A raft is made by tying a platform onto objects that float well, or are buoyant. The raft shown here is easy to make with everyday materials. If you do not have large inner tubes, you could use large airtight containers to make the raft buoyant.

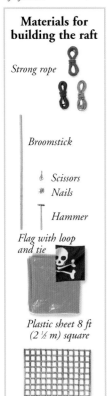

Materials for building the raft

Strong rope

Broomstick

Scissors

Nails

Hammer

Flag with loop and tie

Plastic sheet 8 ft (2 ½ m) square

Trellis 6 ½ ft (2 m) square

Four large inner tubes

Making your raft

This raft will carry two people on a lake. Never take it out on open water, and always be sure an adult is nearby.

1 Arrange the four inner tubes in a square shape. Tie the tubes together with pieces of rope and secure the rope with reef knots.

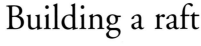

Put a half-hitch knot in each end of the rope to stop the ends from fraying.

See page 39 learn how t a reef knot a half-hitch kn

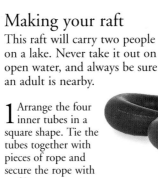

You could use a piece of lightweight plywood instead.

2 Lay the trellis the top of the tubes. Make sure trellis sits squarely

Ideally, the fou inner tubes sh larger than th

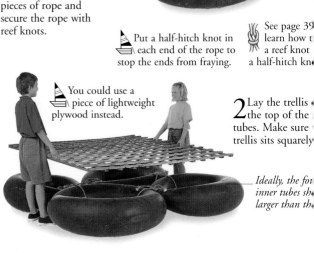

3 Attach the trellis to the inner tubes by wrapping a piece of rope around each inner tube and section of trellis in turn.

Make the rope extra secure by knotting it to the trellis with a reef knot at each section.

Weave the rope through the trellis and pull it tight.

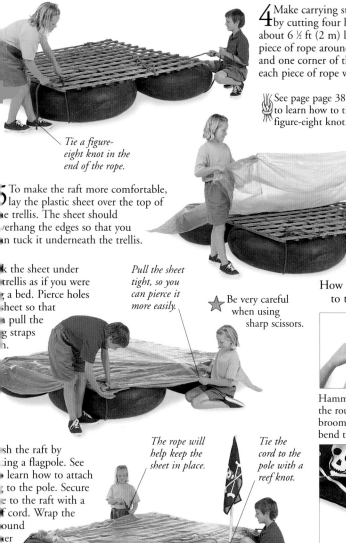

4 Make carrying straps for the raft by cutting four lengths of rope about 6 ½ ft (2 m) long. Loop each piece of rope around an inner tube and one corner of the trellis. Secure each piece of rope with a reef knot.

See page page 38 to learn how to tie a figure-eight knot.

Tie a figure-eight knot in the end of the rope.

5 To make the raft more comfortable, lay the plastic sheet over the top of the trellis. The sheet should overhang the edges so that you can tuck it underneath the trellis.

...k the sheet under trellis as if you were ...g a bed. Pierce holes ...sheet so that ...pull the ...g straps ...

Pull the sheet tight, so you can pierce it more easily.

★ Be very careful when using sharp scissors.

...sh the raft by ...ing a flagpole. See ...learn how to attach ...to the pole. Secure ...e to the raft with a ...f cord. Wrap the ...ound ...er ...d ...nt ...rellis.

The rope will help keep the sheet in place.

Tie the cord to the pole with a reef knot.

How to attach the flag to the broomstick

Hammer a nail into the rounded end of the broomstick. Carefully bend the nail over.

Hook the flag's looped end over the nail and tie the other end to the stick.

...ng afloat

...must always ...first when you ...r the water. ...f you are a ...ent swimmer, ...wear a life jacket. ...a muscle cramp ...eak accident, you ...know when you ...ed the help ...otation aid.

This life jacket supports your entire torso and fits just like a vest.

The large armholes make it comfortable to wear.

The buoyancy on a life jacket like this one is at the front, so you float on your back.

Blow through this tube to inflate the life jacket further.

Steering your raft

Use the carrying straps on your raft to take it to the water's edge.

Floating on a homemade raft is easy and fun. Steering the raft is harder because it [has] a flat bottom, and it can be blown acros[s] the water by the wind. It is important therefore to use your raft only on very calm water. Punting and paddling are the best ways to steer your raft.

Materials for steering your raft

Pole about 6 ½ ft (2 m) long

Cutting board

Cord

Pole about 1 ½ ft (½ m) long

Pole about 10 ft (3 m) long

Nails

Colored tape

Hammer

Hints and tips

Decorate your punt pole with strips of the colored tape.

To paddle forward, both people must paddle together. If you paddle out of time, you will move around in circles.

Punting your raft

Punting is when you use a long pole to push your raft along. You can only punt in fairly shallow water.

Use the longes[t] pole as your punt pole.

1 Stand at the back of your raft with the punt pole. Hold the pole one third of the way from the top.

2 Lower the punt pole to the lake bottom. Now push the end of the pole away from you to move the raft forward.

3 Bend over and grip the lower end of the pole with one hand. Lift the pole up out of the water, ready to perform the next stroke.

Twist the pole sligh[tly] before you lift it to make sure it does n[ot] get stuck on the lake botton.

Pivot the pole on your thigh.

4 To steer the raft, use the po[le] like a rudder. Hold the pole at an angle. Bend your knee slightly and rest t[he] pole against it. Push th[e] pole behind you to steer the raft to the left and in fron[t] of you to steer to the right.

to make a paddle
a cutting board
d two poles

 small loop in
d of the cord and
it with a figure-
not.

 pole that is
2 m) long. Tie the
l end of the cord to
e with a reef knot.

rd should be about
) cm) from the end
ole. Lay the short
cord along the pole.

he cord around
 until you have
 about 3 in
of the pole.

g the wrapped
curely, thread the
d of the cord
 the looped end.

page 38 to
n how to tie
igure-eight knot
ge 39 to tie a reef
d half-hitch knot.

Paddling your raft

Once you have made two
paddles, try paddling
your raft. Kneel on either
side of the raft so that
it is balanced.

You need two
people to
paddle the raft.

*Kneel down
so that you
can lean
forward as
you paddle.*

1 To move forward, push the paddles through
the water from the front to the back of the
raft. Lift the paddles out of the water, bring
them back to the front, and start again.

*Put the blade
squarely in the
water and push it
away from you.*

2 To turn the raft, sit at
opposite corners. The
front paddler sweeps the
paddle blade through the
water in a large arc to the
back of the raft. The back
paddler uses her paddle
as a rudder.

*Sweep the
paddle to the
back of the raft.*

3 When both
paddles have been pushed
through the water as far as
possible, the raft will have
done a quarter-turn.

*Wrap cord at each
end of the paddle
blade to make it
extra secure.*

How to make a paddle for your raft (continued)

Secure the cord by
threading it through one
wrapped piece and tying
two half-hitch knots.

Repeat these steps half-
way down the pole to
make another hand grip
for your paddle.

Lay the cutting board
over the end of the
pole that has no
wrapped cord.

Lay the shortest pole over
the cutting board and
longest pole. Nail all
three pieces together.

Secure the paddle blade
by wrapping cord around
both ends of the two poles.
Secure with reef knots.

★ If you have not
used a hammer
before, ask an adult
to show you how.

Open canoes seat several people and are the most popular kind of canoe.

Equipment

Paddles

Open canoe

Canoeing with friends

An open canoe can seat at least three peopl making it perfect for group adventures. It usually moved through the water with two paddles – one person paddles at the front, bow, of the canoe on one side, and a secor person paddles at the back, or stern, of the canoe on the opposite side.

Stepping in

The golden rule for getting into an open canoe is to step in one person at a time.

Always wear a life jacket when canoeing.

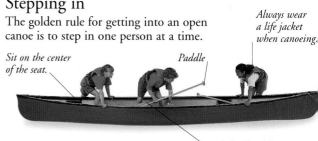

Sit on the center of the seat.

Paddle

Blade of paddle

Paddling forward

You can either sit or kneel in the canoe. Kneeling on one knee will give you more control. Keep your body-weight in the center of the boat and try not to lean over the side, or gunwale.

See pag learn hold the p correctly.

Gunwale   *Grip*   *Shaft*

1 If you are paddling on the right, hold the paddle grip with your left hand and the shaft with your right hand. Do the opposite f the left side. Lean forward and put the blade squarely in the water.

2 Pull the blade through the water to the back of the canoe. Benc the arm on the paddling side and pull it toward your chest. You lower arm and back should provide most of the pulling power.

3 Lift the blade up out of the water and bring it to the front of the boat. You are now ready to perform another stroke. Remember to make sure the blade goes squarely into the water.

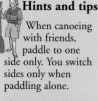

Hints and tips

When canoeing with friends, paddle to one side only. You switch sides only when paddling alone.

Both paddlers should coordinate their strokes in order to move the canoe in a straight line.

ow to hold an
open canoe
ddle correctly

he hand opposite
addling side on the
url your fingers
e top of the grip.

he hand on your
ng side around the
our hands should
ulder-width apart.

sh forward with
ur lower hand
ide the paddle
ur upper hand.

Paddling backward

To paddle backward in a straight line, make sure both paddlers perform each stroke at the same time.

Remember to look behind you often to see where you are going.

1 Put the blade of the paddle squarely into the water behind you. Twist your body from the hips to gain more pushing power and grip the paddle firmly.

2 Push the paddle through the water as far as you can. Now lift the paddle up out of the water and bring it toward the stern to do the next stroke.

Stopping quickly
Paddle in the opposite direction to stop your canoe. If you are moving forward, paddle backward.

ut turn

sweep stroke to turn around.
the canoe is being turned
vise, or to the right. Do
pposite to turn left.

1 The back paddler puts her blade in the water near the stern and sweeps it in a wide arc to the bow. The front paddler does the opposite.

Make sure the shaft does not go below the water.

The front paddler sweeps the paddle in a large arc from the bow to the stern.

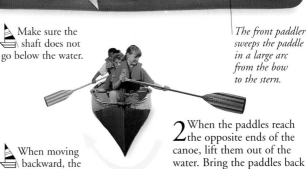

and left turns
e back paddle to steer
oe when you are moving
d. To move to your right,
he blade away from you.
ve to your left, pull
de toward you.

When moving backward, the front paddler steers.

2 When the paddles reach the opposite ends of the canoe, lift them out of the water. Bring the paddles back to their starting positions.

ke sure each
de is square to
ter and repeat
roke until you
urned the
around.

Kayaking is fun to do with friends, so try to get a group together.

Steering a kayak

A canoe with a closed top is called a kayak. Originally kayaks were used in very cold or rough water, where open canoes would probably fill with water. Nowadays kayaks used on calm water, too. This is the best p to learn to paddle in them – it takes practi to learn how to balance and steer a kayak.

Equipment

Paddle

Kayak

Getting afloat

To get the kayak into the water, hold the cockpit with both hands. Keep your back straight, bend your legs, and lower the kayak into the water.

If the kayak fee too heavy for y ask an adult to lowe into the water inste

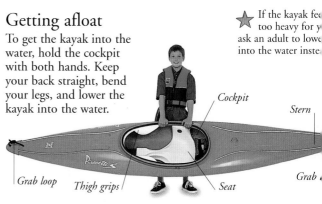

Cockpit

Stern

Grab loop *Thigh grips* *Seat* *Grab*

Sliding in

It is important to slide into the kayak smoothly. If you hesitate halfway, the kayak could slide away from you when you are not fully in it.

Always wear a life jacket when kayaking.

Place the paddle on the bank within easy reach of the kayak.

Keep your body-weight low.

1 Crouch down an hold the bank wi one hand and the b the cockpit rim with other. Put one foot the center of the co

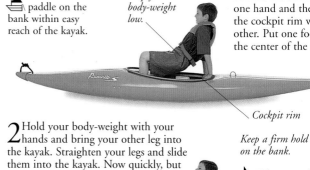

Cockpit rim

2 Hold your body-weight with your hands and bring your other leg into the kayak. Straighten your legs and slide them into the kayak. Now quickly, but carefully, sit down.

Keep a firm hold on the bank.

When seated, o your legs so th rest on the thigh gr either side of the ka

Butt your feet up to the footrest inside the kayak.

Hints and tips

You could ask an adult to hold the kayak close to the water's edge when you first get in.

To get out of a kayak reverse the steps to get in.

Use the grab loops to tow or carry the kayak.

Using your paddle

The blades of a paddle are at right angles to each other, or feathered, so you need to twist the shaft with one hand during each stroke.

See left for help choosing which hand to twist when paddling.

Shaft

Grip the shaft with your hands shoulder-width apart.

Blade

Paddling forward

Forward paddling requires practice before you'll go in a straight line.

1 Reach forward from the hips with the left-hand blade. Keep your body-weight central and put the blade squarely in the water.

Here, the left hand is the control hand.

The blade should be fully in the water.

2 Keep the blade alongside, or parallel, to the kayak and pull it through the water to the back of the kayak.

3 Lift the blade out of the water. Twist the shaft with the control hand, so the right-hand blade is square to the water. Lean forward with the right-hand blade and do a stroke on this side in exactly the same way.

Paddle evenly on both sides to move forward in a straight line.

...lling backward

...troke is just the opposite of ...ing forward, but a little harder ...fect. You need to twist ...ody more and ...ehind you ...rly to check ...you are going.

1 Twist from your hips and put the right-hand blade squarely in the water behind you. Push the blade toward the front of the kayak.

Guide the left-hand blade with your left hand.

2 Lift the right-hand blade out of the water and twist the shaft with your control hand, so the left-hand blade is square to the water. You are now ready to put this blade in the water at the back of the kayak and perform another stroke.

Remember to keep the blade parallel to the kayak.

[left column fragments]

...v to figure out ...h hand to twist ...en you paddle

...overhand grip to ...e paddle. Keep ...umbs underneath ...ft.

...e shaft firmly ...ne hand, here the ...d, and loosely ...e other.

...he shaft with ...ipped hand. ...rip and twist ...ur opposite ...The hand that ...ost comfortably ...control hand.

Kayak adventures

Kayaks come in many shapes and sizes, ea[ch] suited for a different activity or adventure. White-water kayaks are long and thin, and canoe polo kayaks are short, with rounder ends. Despite these differences, all kayaks are long and narrow, which makes them very easy to overturn, or capsize.

When you first start kayaking, you will use a general-purpose kayak.

Capsizing a kayak

One of the first skills to learn is how to capsize safely in a kayak. This is best done in a swimming pool with a qualified instructor.

Always wear a life jacket, even when in a swimming pool.

1 Give your paddle to t[he] instructor. Prepare yo[ur] for the capsize by tak[ing] a deep breath and p[ut] firmly on the thigh

2 Grip the sides of the kayak with your arms and lean over to one side. The kayak will capsize.

3 Wait until you are completely upsid[e] down in the water before trying to g[et] out. Tap the underside of the kayak thr[ee] times, then put your hands on either si[de] of the cockpit rim, close to your hips.

4 Keeping your legs straight, lift up and push yourself forward out of the kayak. Make sure you keep your head tucked in.

Tap the bottom of the kayak before getting out to show that you have not been injured during the capsize.

5 As you leave the cockpit, gently roll forward. Once you are completely out, swim to the surface. Hold a grab loop and tow the capsized kayak to the poolside. Once you are out of the pool, the instructor will help you empty the kayak of water.

...ning your kayak

...inal skill you need to master
...on is turning your kayak.
...easiest way to do this is by
...rming a sweep stroke.

1 To turn counterclockwise, lean forward
from your hips and put the right-hand
blade squarely in the water. Push
down on your right foot
to help with the stroke.

*...y to keep
...ur body-weight
...tral rather than
...ning to one side.*

2 With the paddle just below the water's surface,
sweep it in a wide arc from the front to the back
of the kayak. Twist your shoulders around
with your hips and try to keep your
sweeping arm straight.

*Keep the
blade square
in the water.*

*... turn clockwise,
...e right-hand
...sweeps from
...o front, and the
...nd blade sweeps
...ront to back.*

3 When the blade is as close to the
back as possible, lift it out of the
water. Twist the shaft with your
control hand so that
the left-hand blade
is square to the water.

*...sh down with
...ur left foot when
...eping with the
...-hand blade.*

4 Put the left-hand blade in the
water at the back and sweep it
around to the front in a wide
arc. Repeat this process until
your kayak has turned.

Hints and tips

...ways tow your
...yak upside down.
...you try to turn it
...ght way up in the
...it will fill with
...and may sink.

...yak slalom
...acing involves
...ng in and out of
...s of obstacles as
...you can paddle.

...he course of a
...ayak marathon
...e as long as
...iles (193 km)!

Different kinds of kayaks

Kayak activities are so varied that
everyone can find something
they enjoy. Once you have
mastered your skills in a
general-purpose kayak, you
could try slalom racing
or even surf kayaking!

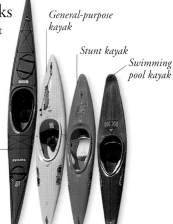

*General-purpose
kayak*

Stunt kayak

*Swimming
pool kayak*

Sea kayak

A sea kayak
is long and
thin so that you
can cut through
waves quickly
without capsizing.

Planning a canoeing tri[

Having learned how to canoe, you could g
on a canoeing day trip with your local boa
club. Planning is the key to any successful
trip. Your canoeing instructor should plan
your route and check your canoe and padd
are in good condition. It is up to you to be
sure you properly pack gear and provisions

You can go on a day trip in either a kayak or an open canoe.

Materials to waterproof your gear

String

Cord

Plastic bag

Garbage bag

🛶 Hints and tips

Tying your gear to the kayak keeps it in place. It also safeguards against losing your gear if you capsize.

🛶 If your kayak has a single piece of string instead of a securing loop, tie your gear to it with a sheet bend knot. See page 41 to learn how to tie a sheet bend knot.

🛶 Wear sun block on hot days.

Being prepared

Pack these items to make sure you are prepared for anything.

First aid kit

Hat to protect you from the sun

Spare shoes

Waterproof top

Swimsuit

Pack a sweatshirt in case you get cold.

Sweatshirt

Shorts

A pair of shorts will help keep you cool on a hot day.

Towel

Sweatpants

You could pack warm, lightweight pants instead of sweatpants.

How to waterp[
your clothes and a
them to your ka

Put your clothes in
plastic bag. Roll the
and clothes, pushin[
any extra air in the

Seal the plastic bag
tying a knot in it. A
hitch knot will be t
easiest one to tie.

Tie 1 ½ ft (50 cm) c
string around the k[
bag. Secure the stri[
with a reef knot.

Wrap the string arou
the bag to keep it t[
rolled so that it will
inside the kayak eas

v to waterproof
your clothes
(continued)

he bag down the
the kayak cockpit.
ne end of the bag
he seat.

string on the bag
securing loop on
ak with a round
d two half-hitches.

page 39 to
n how to tie
ef knot and
d turn and
f-hitches.

ayak has
space on either
the cockpit.

Your packed lunch

Paddling a canoe all day can be tiring and will certainly make you hungry, so always take a packed lunch. Choose food that is easy to carry and that will not spoil if it is a warm day.

Keep your food fresh and water-proof by packing it in an airtight container.

Fruit is very refreshing and easy to carry.

Chips are a tasty way to end your meal.

Always take plenty to drink.

Sandwiches are filling and easy to pack.

A chocolate bar is full of sugar, which will give you energy.

Packing your gear

Whatever you take with you will be stored in your canoe. This will make the craft heavier and harder to paddle, so only pack what you really need.

Store your gear as close to the cockpit as possible.

Storage space on either side of the cockpit

Buoyancy block

Buoyancy block helps keep the kayak afloat.

ing a sail

set off in an open canoe, pack
garbage bag and some string
ke a sail. Follow the instructions
for making a sail. You
en sit back and let
nd blow you along
rt of your trip.

Hold the sail close to the lashed section.

See page 41 to learn how to tie shear lashing.

ave a spare
you can
s a rudder.

the two paddles.
or lash, them together
with shear lashing
he shaft of the paddle.

2 Pull the ends of the paddles apart to form a cross shape. This cross should be large enough to fill the garbage bag.

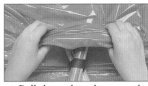

3 Pull the garbage bag over the crossed paddles to make the sail. Kneeling in the middle of the canoe, hold the sail upright.

A rowboat seats up to three people, so you can take turns rowing.

Rowing a boat

Learning to row a boat takes some practic because you row facing backward. This means that each maneuver is always the opposite of what you would expect it to b When you first start rowing, concentrate (performing each stroke smoothly and lool behind you often to see where you are goi

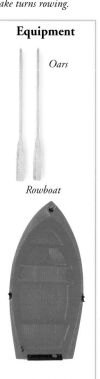

Equipment

Oars

Rowboat

Setting off
Make sure that the rowboat is tied up, or moored. Step into the boat from the moored end gripping both sides of the boat for balance.

Step into the center of the boat.

Rowing forward
You move a rowboat by rowing with a pair of oars. To go forward, face the stern of the boat and push it forward with the oars.

Sit squarely on the center seat.

Keep the oars close to the side of the boat.

Oars and oarlock
The oarlock on the of the boat helps k the oar in the right position for rowing

1 Put the blade of each in the water behind y toward the bow of the boa Lean forward from your hips and brin your arms straight out in front of you.

Keep your back straight.

Bring your close to you

Holding the oars
The end of each oar has a specially shaped hand grip. Hold the oars with an overhand grip.

Imagine the oars are moving in a circle parallel to the sides of the boat.

2 Bend your arms and pull them up toward you. This will bring the blades of the oars through the water to the center of the boat.

The thin e the blade sl be alongside parallel to,

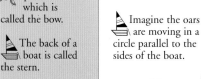

3 Lift the oars up (the water. Sweep toward to the bow (boat. You are now r to start a new stroke

...ing your boat

...you turn your boat, imagine
...e using the oars to push and
...through the water.

...will need
...perform
...ke about
...es to
...full turn.

1 To move the
boat to your
right, point the blade
of your right-hand oar toward the stern
and the blade of your left-hand oar to the bow.

*Slide the thin side
of the blade into
the water first.*

*Try to stay seated in
the center of the boat.*

2 Move the oars through
the water. Push the right-
hand oar away from you
and pull the left-hand
oar toward you.

*Keep the blade square in the water
so you have as much pushing and
pulling power as possible.*

*Twist your
body from
the hips.*

...ow the boat will have turned
...tly. Lift the oars parallel to
...s of the boat, ready to sweep
...ross the top of the water.

*Make sure the flat edge of the blade is
at right angles to the boat. This will make
it easier to put the blade back in the water.*

4 Bring the oars to the opposite ends
of the boat – the right-hand blade
pointing to the stern and the left-
hand blade pointing to the bow.
Put the blades back in the water
and perform the next stroke.

...ring a rowboat

...you have finished using your
...lways remember to tie it up,
...r it. The rope that you
...he boat with is called
...er line. Tie this rope
...cure object, such as
...ing ring or post.

See page 39 to
learn how to tie
a round turn and
two half-hitches.

*The painter
line is attached
to the boat
with a figure-
eight knot.*

*Place the handle-
ends of the oars
inside the boat.*

...e this end of the
...inter line to a secure
...ject with a round turn
...d two half-hitches.

An Optimist is so easy to sail you can go out on your own.

What is an Optimist?

An Optimist is a small sailboat. There are many different kinds of small sailboats, b the Optimist is the simplest and easiest to learn to sail in. An Optimist can be operated by one or two people and has all the basic equipment found on larger and more complicated sailboats.

The parts of a sailboat

All sailboats have certain features in common. Study the ones shown here to learn the names of the different parts.

Always wear a life jacket when in the boat.

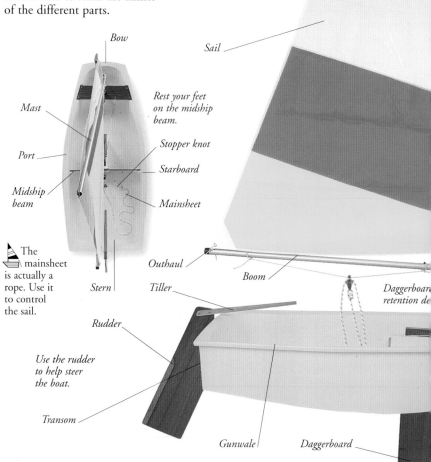

Bow

Sail

Mast

Rest your feet on the midship beam.

Port

Stopper knot

Starboard

Midship beam

Mainsheet

The mainsheet is actually a rope. Use it to control the sail.

Outhaul

Boom

Daggerboar retention de

Stern

Tiller

Rudder

Use the rudder to help steer the boat.

Transom

Gunwale

Daggerboard

‍paring to set sail

‍ easiest way to get into an Optimist
‍m a bank. However, if you set sail
‍allow water you will need to push
‍oat out into the water, making sure
‍aggerboard and rudder are in the
‍ Once in deep enough water,
‍an climb in.

‍hen you are on a bank,
‍ into the boat from the
‍ or side – whichever is
‍t to the bank. Hold the
‍n one hand and the
‍ ale with the other. Step
‍he center of the boat.

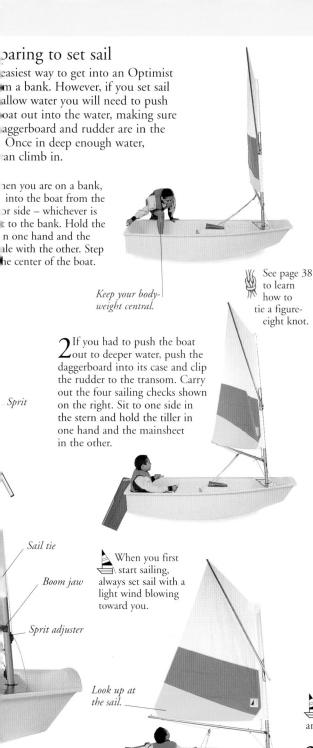

Keep your body-weight central.

Sprit

2 If you had to push the boat
out to deeper water, push the
daggerboard into its case and clip
the rudder to the transom. Carry
out the four sailing checks shown
on the right. Sit to one side in
the stern and hold the tiller in
one hand and the mainsheet
in the other.

See page 38
to learn
how to
tie a figure-
eight knot.

Sail tie

Boom jaw

Sprit adjuster

When you first
start sailing,
always set sail with a
light wind blowing
toward you.

*Look up at
the sail.*

‍he daggerboard
‍ lps stop the boat
‍ m drifting
‍ deways.

Four important checks
to carry out before
you set sail

Make sure the sprit is
pulled up tightly in the
V-shaped sprit adjuster,
which is on the mast.

The mainsheet should
have a stopper knot tied
in it. This knot is usually
a figure-eight.

Once in the boat, make
sure the daggerboard is
slotted into place with
its retention device.

Check the rudder is
properly and securely
clipped to the transom
at the stern of the boat.

Use the mainsheet
to let the sail out
and pull the sail in.

3 You are now ready
to set sail. Pull the
mainsheet in so that the
sail fills out and push the
tiller away from you. You
should now move off.

Sailing upwind

When you first start sailing, make sure there is an onshore wind, and start sailing upwind. If you get into trouble you can then let go of everything in the boat and be blown back to land.

When you sail upwind, you are sailing into the wind.

The about the w

When you are facing directly into the wind, the sail will flap loosely.

2 To move the boat straight ahead, you will need to turn it. Push the tiller away from you and start pulling in the mainsheet. You are now sailing as close to the wind as you can. This is called beating.

3 If you continue beating, you will sail forward, but will still move to the side. To go straight, duck down and pull the mainsheet toward you. The boom will cross over to the other side of the boat.

When you are beating with the wind on the port side, you are doing a port beat.

The sail is now swinging to the port side

Switching sides in the boat is called tacking.

Let the sail fill out with the wind.

Prepare to duck under the boom.

4 Once the boom has swung to the other side, sit down across from it. Switch your hands over on the tiller and mainsheet. Start to pull in the mainsheet and straighten the tiller.

Hints and tips

When the wind blows toward the land, it is called an onshore wind.

A tack also describes the direction, or line, the boat is traveling. In step one, the boat is reaching on a port tack, and in step five it is on a starboard tack.

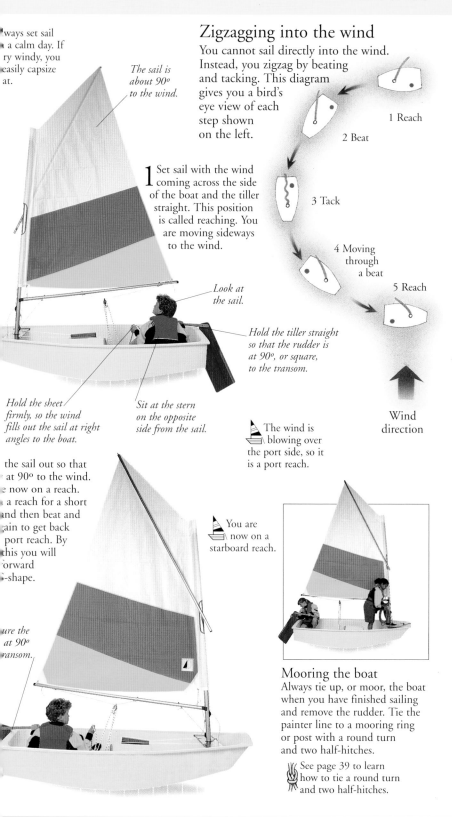

ways set sail
a calm day. If
ry windy, you
easily capsize
at.

*The sail is
about 90°
to the wind.*

Zigzagging into the wind

You cannot sail directly into the wind.
Instead, you zigzag by beating
and tacking. This diagram
gives you a bird's
eye view of each
step shown
on the left.

1 Reach

2 Beat

1 Set sail with the wind
coming across the side
of the boat and the tiller
straight. This position
is called reaching. You
are moving sideways
to the wind.

3 Tack

4 Moving
through
a beat

5 Reach

*Look at
the sail.*

*Hold the tiller straight
so that the rudder is
at 90°, or square,
to the transom.*

*Hold the sheet
firmly, so the wind
fills out the sail at right
angles to the boat.*

*Sit at the stern
on the opposite
side from the sail.*

The wind is
blowing over
the port side, so it
is a port reach.

Wind
direction

the sail out so that
at 90° to the wind.
now on a reach.
a reach for a short
and then beat and
ain to get back
port reach. By
this you will
orward
-shape.

You are
now on a
starboard reach.

ure the
at 90°
ransom.

Mooring the boat

Always tie up, or moor, the boat
when you have finished sailing
and remove the rudder. Tie the
painter line to a mooring ring
or post with a round turn
and two half-hitches.

See page 39 to learn
how to tie a round turn
and two half-hitches.

Sailing downwind

Moving downwind is easier than sailing upwind. The quickest way to turn around after sailing upwind is by performing a jibe. Having done this, you can sail downwind back to land by running.

You should only ever sail in light winds, especially when jibing.

Turning away from the wind

With the wind behind you and the sail out at 90°, you will be running straight back to land. This diagram gives you a bird's eye view of each step shown on the right to steer into this position.

6 Running

5 Finishing the jibe

4 Jibing

3 Preparing to jibe

2 Run

1 Reach

Wind direction

4 Pull the tiller all the way toward you. This will make the sail swing over to the other side of the boat.

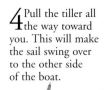

3 To turn the boat back to land, prepare to jibe. Duck down, ready to move under the boom. Start bringing the tiller gently toward you.

Keep your head down.

Keep hold of the mainsheet.

You are now ready to perform a jibe.

2 When the sail is out at 90° to the wind and the tiller is pulled slightly toward you, you will be on a run.

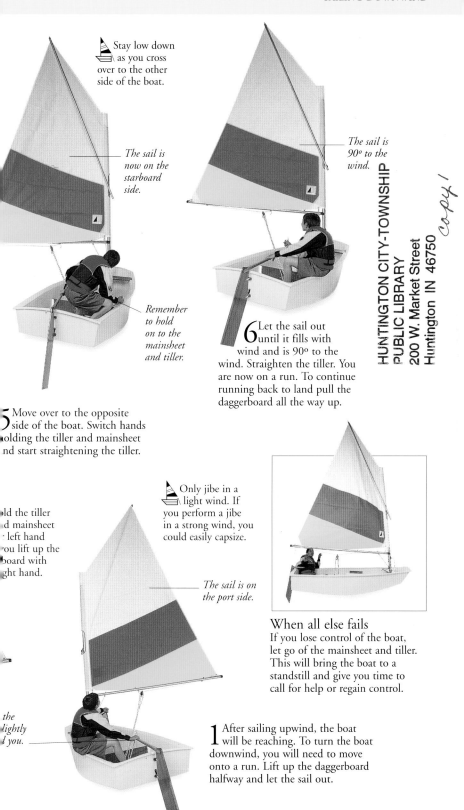

Stay low down as you cross over to the other side of the boat.

The sail is now on the starboard side.

Remember to hold on to the mainsheet and tiller.

The sail is 90° to the wind.

6 Let the sail out until it fills with wind and is 90° to the wind. Straighten the tiller. You are now on a run. To continue running back to land pull the daggerboard all the way up.

5 Move over to the opposite side of the boat. Switch hands holding the tiller and mainsheet and start straightening the tiller.

Hold the tiller and mainsheet left hand you lift up the board with ght hand.

Only jibe in a light wind. If you perform a jibe in a strong wind, you could easily capsize.

The sail is on the port side.

the lightly you.

When all else fails
If you lose control of the boat, let go of the mainsheet and tiller. This will bring the boat to a standstill and give you time to call for help or regain control.

1 After sailing upwind, the boat will be reaching. To turn the boat downwind, you will need to move onto a run. Lift up the daggerboard halfway and let the sail out.

Maps and charts

When planning a day trip, you must have a good knowledge of the area. Largeboat sailors often use a kind of map called a ch to gain this knowledge. A chart shows the depth of the water, any underwater hazard and navigation points. Smallboat sailors, however, only need a map to refer to.

It is important to know the depth of the water so you do not run aground.

Materials for the bag of shot

Rubber bands *Scissors*

Pebbles

Square of material

Plastic bags

Rope

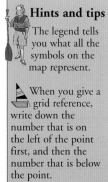

Hints and tips

The legend tells you what all the symbols on the map represent.

When you give a grid reference, write down the number that is on the left of the point first, and then the number that is below the point.

Legend

═══	*Major road*
───	*Minor road*
⋊⋉	*Bridge*
⬭	*Lake*
⬯	*Reservoir*
⌒	*River*
▲	*Forest*
⋎	*Marsh*
—200—	*Contour line*

Water-depth bands
0–150 ft
150–300 ft
300–450 ft
450–600 ft
Over 600 ft

Water-depth bands

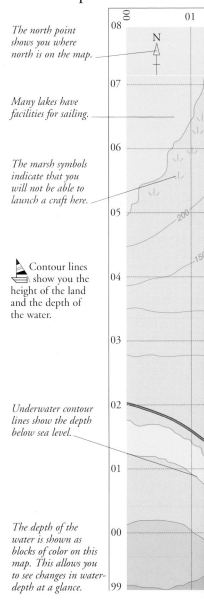

The north point shows you where north is on the map.

Many lakes have facilities for sailing.

The marsh symbols indicate that you will not be able to launch a craft here.

Contour lines show you the height of the land and the depth of the water.

Underwater contour lines show the depth below sea level.

The depth of the water is shown as blocks of color on this map. This allows you to see changes in water-depth at a glance.

v to read a map

p gives you all the information that a small boat
needs to plan a day trip. It has a legend to explain
mbols, contour lines to indicate the height of the
and a north point to show you where north is on
ap. This map also shows you the depth of the water.

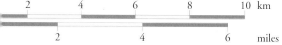

2   4   6   8   10 km

2   4   6   miles

bar

thing on a map is scaled down and drawn to a fraction of
l size. On this map the scale is 1:50,000. This means that
2 cm) on the map is equal to ⅔ mile (1 km) on the ground.

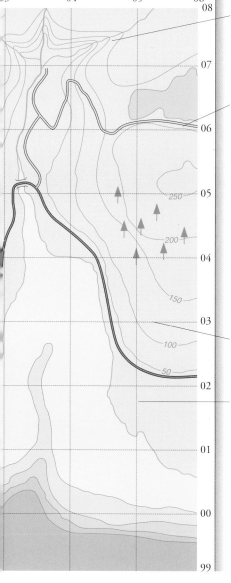

03   04   05   06

08
07
06
250 — 05
200 — 04
150
03
100
50
02
01
00
99

*These closely
spaced contour
lines show that the
river is running
down too steep a
hill for canoeing.*

*This minor
road gives access
to the reservoir.*

Most maps
have a grid of
squares on them.
The lines are
drawn at regular
intervals and are
all numbered.
This allows you to
refer to any point
on the map giving
these numbers.

*The grid lines that
run across the map
are called northings.*

*The grid lines that
run down the map
are called eastings.*

Lower the
"bag" into the
water until it hits
the bottom. Count
the number of
knots in the water
to measure the
depth in feet.

How to make a bag of shot to measure the depth of water

Put two handfuls of
pebbles on the material.
Wrap the material around
the pebbles.

Secure the material
around the pebbles with a
rubber band. You now
have a bag of shot.

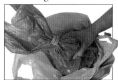

Put the shot in a plastic
bag and seal the bag with
a rubber band. Place this
bag in a second bag.

The shot is now water-
proof. Tie the rope to the
handles of both plastic
bags with a reef knot.

Tie figure-eight knots in
the rope at 3-ft (1-m)
intervals. This rope will
measure the water depth.

See page 39 to
learn how to tie a
reef knot and
page 38 to tie a
figure-eight knot.

You should always check that all the knots on your boat are tied correctly.

Useful nautical knots I

There are many different kinds of boating or nautical, knots, each with a specific use It is just as important to learn the uses and strengths of particular knots as it is to kno how to tie them correctly. For example, a round turn and two half-hitches jams und strain, so it is a very good mooring knot.

Materials

Ropes of varying thicknesses

Hints and tips

Tying a double figure-eight knot is a very quick way to put a loop in a piece of rope.

To stop a natural-fiber rope from fraying, tie a half-hitch knot in each end.

An artificial-fiber rope will not rot as easily as a natural-fiber rope.

A natural-fiber rope is easier to handle than an artificial-fiber rope when it is wet and icy.

Tying a figure-eight knot

This knot enlarges the end of a rope. It stops the end from running through a ring or pulley.

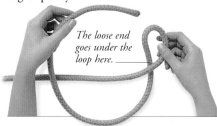

The loose end goes under the loop here.

1 Imagine one end of the rope is attached to a sail. Make a loop with the loose end of rope. Bring this end under and over the loop.

2 Bring the loose end through the loop. Hold the attached end of the rope in one hand to keep the loop secure.

3 Pull both ends of the rope to tighten the knot. Whenever you go sailing, make sure the ends of all the sheets have a figure-eight knot.

How to tie a do figure-eight kn a piece of rope

Double over a piec rope. Make a loop wherever you want to be in the rope.

Wrap the looped e rope up and around loose ends in a figu eight shape.

Bring the looped e down through the lowest loop in the figure-eight shape.

Pull the ends tight. You now have a ver secure loop in the of your rope.

to tie a half-hitch
ot in a piece of
tring or rope

is knot to tie up
ends. Start by
g a medium-sized
n the rope.

the right-hand side
rope around to the
f the loop and
hrough the loop.

oth ends of the rope
o secure the knot.
not is used to start
other knots.

Tie half-hitch knots around this end of the rope.

two half-hitch
ots in the rope.
e instructions
for how to
lf-hitch knots.

The half-hitch knots should be as close to the round turns as possible.

nish off the knot
pulling the loose
ght and pushing
alf-hitch knots
together.

Tying a mooring knot

A round turn and two half-hitches is
the most common mooring knot. It
is a very quick knot to tie and untie.

Right-hand end

1 Wrap the rope twice through a mooring
ring or around a post. Bring the right-hand
end of the rope under the left-hand end.

2 Loop the right-hand end through the
left-hand end to secure the two round
turns you have just made.

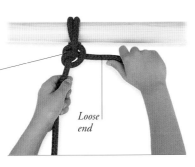

Loose end

Seal a synthetic-
fiber rope by
melting the end with
a match. Always ask
an adult to help
you do this.

A reef knot is a
firm, flat knot
that will not slip
even when it is wet.

How to tie a reef knot
with two pieces of rope
of equal thickness

Get two pieces of rope.
Bring the red piece of
rope over and under the
yellow piece of rope.

Bring the red piece of
rope on the left over the
yellow piece of rope on
the right.

Tuck the red piece of rope
under the yellow piece of
rope. Pull on both pieces
to secure the knot.

It is very easy to undo
this knot. You just push
the two ends of rope
toward each other.

Useful nautical knots II

Any fastening or loop made in string or ro
is generally known as a knot. However, kn
can be divided into smaller more specific
groups. A bend for example, is a knot that
is used to tie two pieces of rope together.
A lashing is another kind of knot, used to
join poles and other long objects together.

*Always keep extra ropes
tidy by coiling them
into neat loops.*

Materials

Rope

Cord

String

Tying a bowline knot

This is the most commonly used
knot for making a loop. It will
not slip or tighten, making it
a very safe loop.

1 Decide how big you want the
finished loop to be. You cannot
change its size once the knot is tied.
Make a small overhand loop and
bring the end back up.

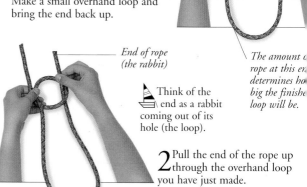

*End of rope
(the rabbit)*

*The amount (
rope at this e
determines ho
big the finishe
loop will be.*

⛵ Think of the
end as a rabbit
coming out of its
hole (the loop).

2 Pull the end of the rope up
through the overhand loop
you have just made.

*Held end
rope (the*

Hints and tips

Make sure that
any rope you use
is not damaged,
or it could easily
break under pressure.

⛵ Most modern
ropes are made
of nylon or polyester.

⛵ Practice tying
each knot at
home so that you can
tie any knot quickly
when you need it.

⛵ Most ropes are
made of three
strands braided
together.

3 Bring the end of the rope
around the back of the held
end of the rope. Now bring
the end around to the front
and down through the loop.

*Pull this
end of the
rope.*

⛵ Imagine the rabbit
goes around the tre
and back into the hole.

4 To finish the knot, pull the
held end of the rope. This
secure the loop. You can also u
this knot to fasten a sheet to a

Tying shear lashing

Shear lashing is a good way to join together long objects that are parallel to, or alongside, each other.

This loop is about 3 in (8 cm) long.

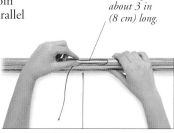

1 Here we are joining two paddles. You will need about 6 ½ ft (2 m) of string. Make a loop in one end of the string and lay it along the top of one of the paddles.

Short end

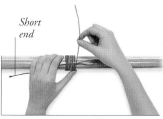

2 Hold the short end of the string firmly in place and wrap the long end of string around the two paddles about ten times.

3 Bring the string through the loop you made at the beginning. Press the wrapped string firmly against the paddles.

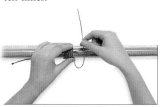

Top end

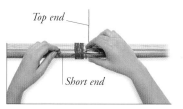

Short end

4 Hold the top end of the string firmly and pull the short end. This will close up the loop and secure the top end of the string.

5 Bring the two ends of the string around to the front of one of the paddles. Push the wrapped string together and keep the loops tight.

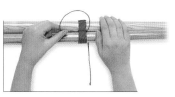

6 Bring one end of the string over to the other side of the wrapped string. Now thread it between the two paddles and around the wrapped string several times. Repeat with the other end of the string.

7 Join the two ends together by tying a reef knot. See page 39 to learn how to tie a reef knot. This kind of lashing is very useful if you want to pull the two objects apart to make an A-frame shape.

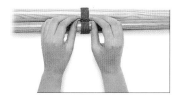

---

to join two ropes equal thickness by a sheet bend knot

a loop in the t piece of rope. ide the thinner f rope through it.

he thin blue ound the back hicker, looped rope.

he end of the blue nderneath the part at crosses the yellow rope.

e end of the blue ht. The two pieces are now securely d together.

nce you have tied knot in a piece e or string, its h will be halved.

ou use artificial-fiber pe on a boat, you ed to wash the rope y to remove any grit.

First aid

When performed with care, most water adventures are very safe. However, it is important to know basic first aid so that you can cope confidently and quickly in an emergency. Always take a first aid kit with you, and make sure you know how to use all the items in it.

Make your first aid kit waterproof by sealing it in an airtight container.

First aid kit

Waterproof bandages to protect cuts and scrapes

Tape to secure gauze bandages

Tweezers to remove insect stings

Safety pins for securing slings

Calamine lotion to soothe sunburned skin

Gauze pad to treat cuts and scrapes

Scissors to cut bandages

Triangular bandage for tying an arm sling

Changing temperatures

When you are outside, your body is more sensitive to changes in temperature. You need to know what to do if you get too hot or too cold.

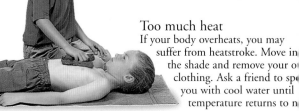

Calamine lotion soothes sunburned skin.

Too much sun

If you have been in the sun too long without suntan lotion, you will get burned. If this happens, move into the shade immediately and apply a soothing cream to the burned skin.

Too much heat

If your body overheats, you may suffer from heatstroke. Move in the shade and remove your o clothing. Ask a friend to sp you with cool water until temperature returns to n

Heatstroke will make you feel dizzy and hot.

If you fe and shi out of th and wa immedi

Not enough sun

If you get very cold and your body temperature falls, you may get hypothermia. This condition can be very dangerous. The most important thing is to heat your body up slowly. Wrap up in warm clothes and blankets, and have a warm drink and some sugary food.

to treat a wasp
g with tweezers
a cold compress

air of tweezers
ove the wasp
Hold the injured
keep it still.

the sting with the
rs as close to the
possible. Pull the
ut carefully.

piece of gauze in
cold water to make
ress. Cool the
th the compress.

ver grasp the
ng at the top
may squeeze
son sac.

Treating a blister

Blisters are very common when doing water sports. If you see a blister developing, stop your activity and treat the blister before it gets any bigger.

A kayaking blister

The most common place to develop blisters when kayaking is at the base of each finger.

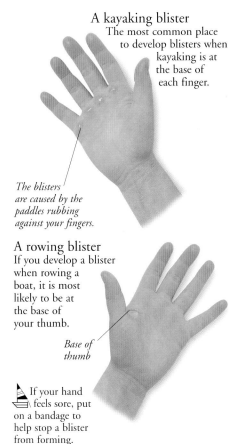

The blisters are caused by the paddles rubbing against your fingers.

A rowing blister

If you develop a blister when rowing a boat, it is most likely to be at the base of your thumb.

Base of thumb

⛵ If your hand feels sore, put on a bandage to help stop a blister from forming.

How to clean and protect a blister with gauze and a bandage

Clean the blister thoroughly with soap and water. Then rinse it with clean, warm water.

For several blisters or one large blister, protect the affected area with a piece of clean gauze.

Lay the gauze over the affected area. Secure the gauze by taping it to the skin.

⛵ Protect a small blister with a bandage that has a pad large enough to cover the affected area.

---

ting cuts and scrapes

you are in the water, a
scrape can easily become
ed. It is therefore important
tect the affected area with
rproof bandage.

1 Gently wash the cut or scrape with a clean gauze pad soaked in clean water. If you do not have a gauze pad, use cotton instead.

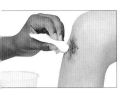

to remove any bits
irt or gravel. Be very
because it may cause
fresh bleeding.

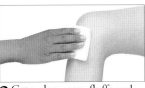

3 Get a clean, non-fluffy pad. Gauze is ideal. Press the pad firmly over the cut or scrape to stop it from bleeding.

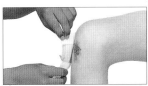

4 Protect the cut or scrape with a waterproof bandage. Choose a bandage with a pad large enough to cover the cut or scrape.

Always wear a life jacket on and near the water.

Water rules

The water is often a busy place, especially on sunny days. To make sure that all your water sports adventures are fun and safe, it is important to remember a few golden rules. When out in a group, always follow the instructions given by the leader and be considerate of other people and animals.

Outdoor Code

All adventurers should know the Outdoor Code. The points shown on these pages are especially important for water sports enthusiasts, so make sure you learn them before you set off.

Take any garbage home or put it in a garbage can. Garbage is not just horrible to look at, it can harm wildlife and plants, too.

If you pass through a gate on your way to the water, leave it as you found it.

Carry your craft along authorized routes, paths, and slipways to the water's edge.

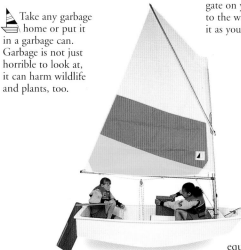

It is very important to make sure that your craft is in good condition and is properly equipped. Always use equipment from a reputable supplier.

Pack a first aid kit and make sure you know how to use it.

Never go on or near the water alone. You must always go out in a group of at least three people. If someone gets hurt, one person can stay with him or her, while another person can go to get help.

Respect wildlife, particularly during breeding seasons. If you get too close to a swan with her cygnets, she may lash out at you.

...ure you know how to ... your watercraft. If you ...busy water, you may ...maneuver out of ...e else's way.

Small boats can be maneuvered much more easily than large boats. If you come across a large boat, always give way to it.

If you want to go swimming or snorkeling, find out when and where it is safe to go.

Observe all warning signs. If you do not, you could find yourself dangerously close to water hazards such as dams.

...t the feelings of the local community. ...often live near the water, so do not ...r make a lot of noise. Keep an eye ...other groups of people and try ...obstruct their course.

Keep away from banks or other areas where people are fishing. If someone is casting, or throwing a fishing line into the water, wait until he or she has done so before passing.

...ays get ...rmission from ...downer before ...n private land.

Always launch and moor your craft at an authorized site, such as a jetty.

...the end of every adventure, ...ays remember to moor ...atercraft securely to a ...g post or ring.

Glossary

Beat
A sailing position in which you sail as close to the wind as possible.

Bow
The front of a canoe, sailboat, or rowboat.

Buoyant
This term is used to describe an item that floats very well.

Capsize
When a boat has overturned in the water it has capsized.

Chart
A water map that shows you the depth of the water, any underwater hazards, and landmarks that will help you find your way, or navigate.

Control hand
The hand that twists the paddle shaft when paddling a kayak.

Daggerboard
A straight board that slots down through the bottom of a sailboat. It helps stop the boat from moving sideways in the water.

Duck-dive
A kind of dive used

when snorkeling to move down through the water.

Fin
The footwear worn when snorkeling. Swimming through the water in fins is called finning.

Gunwale
The upper edge on the hull of a canoe, sailboat, or rowboat. *It is pronounced gunnel.*

Hull
The main body of a canoe, sailboat, or rowboat, including its sides and bottom.

Kayak
A closed canoe that is usually paddled by one person. *It is pronounced kiyak.*

Leeward
The side toward the wind. On a leeward shore, the wind will be blowing from the water to the shore.

Life jacket
A buoyant top that may need to be inflated. In water, a life jacket will help keep you afloat

with your head out of the water.

Mainsheet
The rope that is used to control the sail on a sailboat.

Moor
To tie up a canoe, sailboat, or rowboat to a secure point on land, such as a mooring ring or post.

Oarlock
A horseshoe shaped attachment found on the gunwale of a rowboat. It is used to hold the oar in place.

Port
The left-hand side of a canoe, sailboat, or rowboat when facing the bow.

Reach
A sailing position in which the wind comes from the side of the boat.

Rudder
The blade found at the stern of a sailboat. It is attached to the tiller and helps steer the dinghy.

Run
A sailing positio[n] in which the wi[nd] is directly behin[d] you and the sail is at right angle[s] to the wind.

Sounding
A measurement that shows the depth of the wa[ter.] Soundings are recorded on cha[rts.]

Starboard
The right-hand [side] of a canoe, sailb[oat,] or rowboat whe[n] facing the bow.

Stern
The back of a ca[noe,] sailboat, or rowb[oat.]

Surf kayaking
A sport in whic[h] you surf over wa[ves] in a kayak.

Sweep stroke
A way of turnin[g a] canoe or kayak. [The] blade of the pad[dle] is swept in a lar[ge]

w arc
h the
from one
the canoe or
to the other.

ng position in
the sail is
g from one
the boat
other. This
·n makes the
hange its
on. A tack is
ed to describe
1eral direction

a boat is
traveling in.

Tiller
The lever that is
attached to the
rudder on a
sailboat. The tiller
is pushed and
pulled to move
the rudder, which
steers the boat

Treading water
A way to stay afloat
using as little
energy as possible.

It is an important
water survival
technique. Keeping
yourself upright in
the water, kick down
and out with your
legs and sweep your
arms in front of
you as if you were
doing breaststroke.

Watercraft
A boat of any kind
or several boats.

Windward
The side away

from the wind.
A windward shore
will have the wind
blowing from the
shore to the water.

Useful addresses

The American Athletic Union
c/o Walt Disney World Resort
PO Box 10000
Lake Buena Vista, FL 32830
(407) 363 - 6170

American Sailing Association
13922 Marquesas Way
Marina Del Rey, CA 90292
(310) 822 - 7171

American Sail Training Association
PO Box 1459
Newport, RI 02840
(401) 846 - 1775

Boys & Girls Clubs of America
1230 West Peachtree Street
Atlanta, GA 30309
(404) 815 - 5740

United States Canoe Association
606 Ross Street
Middletown, OH 45044
(513) 422 - 3739

YMCA - National
101 North Wacker Drive
Chicago, IL 60606
(800) 872 - 9622

Scholastic Rowing Association of America
c/o Msgr. Glendon E. Robertson
120 United States Avenue
Gibbsboro, NJ 08026
(609) 784 - 3878

United States Swimming, Inc.
1 Olympic Plaza
Colorado Springs, CO 80909
(719) 578 - 4578

United States Synchronized Swimming
Pan American Plaza
201 South Capitol, Suite 510
Indianapolis, IN 46225
(317) 237 - 5700

United States Water Fitness Association
PO Box 3279
Boynton Beach, FL 33424
(561) 732 - 9908

USA WaterSki
799 Overlook Drive
Winter Haven, FL 33884
(941) 324 - 4341

Index

Acknowledgments

DK would like to thank:

The Islington Boat Club for the use of their
equipment while on location; Paul Anderson
for his invaluable assistance while on location;
Lee Valley Watersports Centre for use of their
reservoir; Whitewater The Canoe Centre for
lending us the open canoe; Perception Kayaks
for lending us the kayaks; Pioneer for lending
us the rowboat; Topper International for
lending us the Optimist; William McManners
for lending us his Jolly Roger flag; Sally
Hamilton for picture research assistance.
Illustrations: Nick Hewetson

Cartography: Jane Voss, David Roberts
Picture research: Mollie Gillard
Picture credits: T top; B below; C center;
L left; R right; A above; B below
The publisher would like to thank the followi
their kind permission to reproduce the photo
Colorsport 44 CR, 45 TL; Natural Image: Mik
45 TR; PPL: John Nash 45 TC; National Trust
Photographic Library: Leo Mason
45 CLB; National Trust Photographic Library:
Ian Shaw 45 CRA; Pyranah 25 BR; Sporting
Pictures (UK) Ltd 45 CRB.